Daniel's Roller Coasters

by Joy Durham Barrett and Lilli Ann Snow

illustrated by Philomena Marano

MODERN CURRICULUM PRESS

Pearson Learning Group

Sixth grader Daniel Gilbert, of Atlanta, Georgia, has an unusual hobby. He designs roller coasters. Of course, his roller coasters aren't the full-size versions that give people thrills and white knuckles. Daniel designs "dream roller coasters" on paper. He often builds three-dimensional models of them too, so that he can better see how they would look if they were really built.

Daniel hopes that someday he will become a designer of real roller coasters. He cannot think of a more exciting job. For now he is doing all the research he can. In fact, Daniel has been studying roller coasters since he was four years old, when he took his first roller coaster ride.

By the age of eight, Daniel had advanced to riding the big-time coasters, including the ones at his favorite park—Six Flags over Georgia. It wasn't long before Daniel was talking and dreaming about roller coasters. Soon he was drawing roller coasters. Then he began to build model roller coasters. Once he built a huge string coaster that stretched across his whole bedroom.

Daniel always has the support of his whole family. His brothers, Josh and Benjamin, and his parents enjoy Daniel's roller coaster projects. And they all ride the big roller coasters with him too.

Daniel's parents help supervise his roller coaster projects. His dad is a civil engineer. A civil engineer designs such things as bridges and roads. His mom is an interior designer. An interior designer designs spaces inside buildings. Daniel grew up watching his parents find one solution after another to different design problems.

Daniel has put a lot of thought into what makes a great roller-coaster ride. He says those things are high speed; big hills with quick, sharp drops; corkscrew turns; fast flips; and good safety features. Other coaster features that Daniel likes are a good "clack-clack-clack sound" and things like waterfalls. In fact, Daniel thinks that the more senses the ride involves, the better.

Daniel knows all about today's roller coasters. And he has also read about early roller coasters.

WHOOSH

The first coasters were not much more than sleds. In Russia in the 1400s, workers built wooden slides on hills and let ice form over them. They carved "sleds" out of blocks of ice, which they used to slide down the ramps. Although the ramps were simple in design, some of them stood over seventy feet tall. And they stretched out for several city blocks!

In the early 1800s, the French copied the Russian idea, adding steel ramps and cars with wheels that locked to their tracks. *Whoosh!* Down the thrill-seekers went—facing sideways!

American designers began building roller coasters in the 1820s. One of the first American coasters was not built for a thrilling ride, but for a coal mine in eastern Pennsylvania.

The workers needed a way to bring heavy coal from the mines in the mountain tops down to the valleys. A car with wheels sitting in the grooves of a track was the perfect answer.

One laborer after another filled the coal cars. Then they gave the cars a push.

Next gravity took over. These "coaster-trains" flew to the bottom of the mountain in about one-half hour, sometimes going faster than a hundred miles an hour.

LEAP THE DIPS, LAKEMONT PARK, ALTOONA, PA.

Some of the first riders on coasters-trains were mules!
The coaster-trains did not have a pulley to hoist them
back up the mountain. So people paid a half dollar, and
climbed aboard the trains, along with mules, for the
quick ride down the mountain. The ride back up on the
mules took almost three hours. It is a good thing that
mules are such strong animals, or they would have
collapsed on the mountain!

One early roller coaster, built in 1902, is still standing in Altoona, Pennsylvania. Today it is the oldest wooden roller coaster in the world. It carried happy riders for eighty-three years until it was closed in 1985. Now it is being repaired and should reopen in time for its hundredth birthday!

When Daniel Gilbert designs a coaster, he thinks of all kinds of roller coasters. First he draws his ideas on paper. He must decide on the angle of the track, because this determines the coaster's speed. He also plans the size and shape of the hills and curves. The coaster must go fast enough to go up the hills, around the curves, and through the loops.

As Daniel studies more about roller coasters, he will learn about the force of gravity, or *g-force*. The g-force tells how much Earth's gravity pushes or pulls a body. Standing on the surface of the Earth, we feel a g-force of one *g*. Most roller coasters have a force of three to four *g*'s. At the bottom of coaster hills and at the top of steel loops, these forces pull downward. These forces are called *positive g*'s.

Daniel likes the feeling of *negative g's* best. We can feel these forces when we ride in a roller coaster's front seat, going uphill, and in the back seat, going downhill. The front and back are Daniel's favorite spots on the coaster, of course! They give him the feeling of floating up out of his seat. Many people think this feeling of weightlessness is a coaster's most thrilling feature.

Daniel is having fun riding coasters and designing small models. But he knows that as a designer of real roller coasters, he would have to design the rides perfectly. "Just one error in a design could hurt someone," he explains.

The most important part of coaster design is safety.
Of course, if a roller coaster collapsed, it would be
terrible. Roller coasters are checked often by medical
doctors and inspectors to be sure that riders will be safe.
These people have machines that measure what
roller-coaster motions do to the human body. The
doctors make sure that riders don't get rocked and
rattled too much.

Roller coasters are given a short safety check every
day. They have more complete checks every six months.

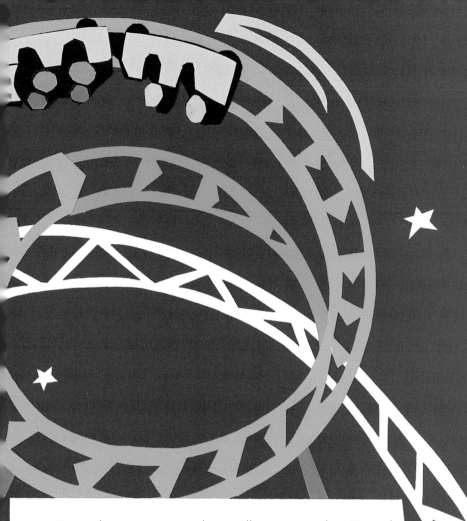

Someday, you may ride a roller coaster that Daniel Gilbert designed. Would you like to know what he'd call it? Right now, he can't tell you. Why?

"First, I'd have to ride it, and learn how it feels. Only after I experienced a ride on it, could I name it properly," he says.

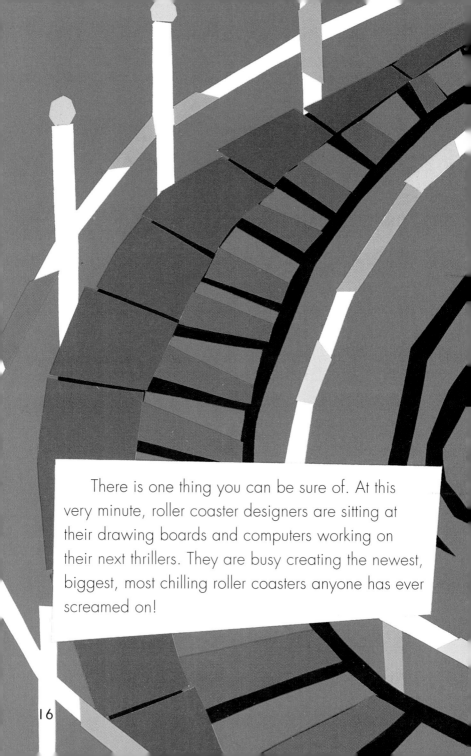

There is one thing you can be sure of. At this very minute, roller coaster designers are sitting at their drawing boards and computers working on their next thrillers. They are busy creating the newest, biggest, most chilling roller coasters anyone has ever screamed on!